JAGGED WITH LOVE

Jagged with Love

Susanna Childress

THE UNIVERSITY OF WISCONSIN PRESS

The University of Wisconsin Press
1930 Monroe Street, 3rd Floor
Madison, Wisconsin 53711-2059
uwpress.wisc.edu

3 Henrietta Street
London WC2E 8LU, England
eurospanbookstore.com

Printed in the United States of America

Library of Congress Cataloging-in-Publication Data
Childress, Susanna.
Jagged with love / Susanna Childress.
p. cm.—(Brittingham prize in poetry)
ISBN 0-299-21260-2 (alk. paper)—ISBN 0-299-21264-5 (pbk. : alk. paper)
I. Title. II. Brittingham prize in poetry (Series)
PS3603.H557J34 2005
811'.6—dc22   2005010079

ISBN-13: 978-0-299-21264-3 (pbk: alk. paper)
ISBN-13: 978-0-299-21263-6 (e-book)

For my mother and Mary Brown, the most remarkable women I know: I want to be both of you when I grow up.

For Derartu Motuma and Mikery Pierre, who will never read this: I thank God for your lives.

contents

III

A RUSH OF BEES

IV

HOUSE OF BREAD

ACKNOWLEDGEMENTS

Grateful acknowledgement is made to the following magazines in which some of the works in this book have appeared, sometimes in slightly different versions or under different titles:

America: "Krash" (June 9–16, 2003)

And Know This Place: Indiana Poetry Anthology: "To Jill Behrman, March 2003"

Apalachee Review: "Across the World a Man Is Lifting His Gun"

Bellingham Review: "Supernova Love Shah" (2002, vol. 25, no. 2, issue 51); "Like the Nudes of Lucian Freud" (2003, vol. 27, nos. 1 & 2, issue 54)

Black Creek Review: "Christmas, 2000" (Summer 2002)

Blackbird: "In Indiana" (Spring 2005, vol. 4, no. 1)

Borderlands: Texas Poetry Review: "The Surgery" (Fall/Winter 2004, no. 23)

Center: "First Child, in the Womb" (2003, vol. 2)

The Cimarron Review: "My Husband Giving Me a Bath" (Spring 2005)

Crab Orchard Review: "Santo Domingo Full of Song" (Summer/Autumn 2004, vol. 9, no. 2)

The Florida Review: "God Is the Dream" (Spring 2004, vol. 29, no. 1)

Fourteen Hills: "Lost in the Cant" (Winter/Spring 2004, vol.10, no. 1)

Fugue: "Prose, I Say, Plasma" (Winter 2005)

Gulf Coast: "Nude Self-Portrait" (Fall 2005)

Image: "Daughter in the Waiting Room"

Indiana Review: "Prose, I Say, Plasma" (Winter 2005)

The Missouri Review: "Jagged with Love," "It's the First Thing," "Muchas Gracias, My Love" (2004, vol. 27, no. 3)

The Mississippi Review: "Sprezzatura" (Spring 2004, vol. 32, nos. 1 & 2)

Nimrod International Journal: "Every Dance with Caroline" (Fall/Winter 2003, vol. 48, no. 1)

Notre Dame Review: "To Prayer," "Just Wanted to Show You a Picture of Myself"

Runes: "Negligee, Negligence, Negligent" (2003)

"We Take the Sky" was part of a collaborative project with Laura Jennings, 2003 Easter Art Exhibit, Hope Chapel, Austin, Texas.

THE AUTHOR WOULD LIKE TO THANK...

The University of Wisconsin Press and Billy Collins; the University of Texas at Austin for the Keene Award, Roy Crane Excellence in Creative Arts Award, and a Michener Thesis Fellowship; and the National Society of Arts and Letters for the 2003 Poetry Award, with special thanks to the San Antonio chapter for their kind selection and support.

Dearest and deepest thanks to my father, mother, sister and brother, who have loved me with such consistency and graciousness I learned what love is; to my mentor, Dr. Mary Brown, whose presence is the quiet touchstone for this manuscript; to David Taylor and the amazing artists at Hope Chapel; to the kind friends and colleagues who have given careful consideration to my work: Barbara Hamby, Sara Pennington, Jennifer Perrine, Jimmy Kimbrell, Nick Allin, Naomi Shihab Nye, Judith Kroll, Steve Gehrke, Jessica Garratt, Phil Pardi, Veronica House, and Carrie Fountain; and finally, to Joshua Banner, God's very keenest gift to me, you are my love poems come true.

I

JUST WANTED TO SHOW YOU A PICTURE OF MYSELF

THIS DAY IS IN LOVE WITH ME

I know because its hands are in my hair and just now I am
        on its mind, it wants to catch me up in it, to please and hold me,
and even with all my dirty pockets turned inside out

it is in desperate love with me, perhaps wants to ravish me,
        makes me smile a little as I walk into the grocery
store. It is enough to hurt Time, hurt him bad. I turn

over a mango and decide to be in love back, yes, in love with you,
        and a small heaven will move, a tree talk, a place underneath me
will open and I'll slip into the ground easily, roll up and down

through layers of loam, pine-needled, silt, bone-buried, the soil
        pushing through my clothes and into me, then shoot up
through a seed, a stamen, a pod. Now, picking

the perfect tomato, I am sure it will hurt Time, he will growl
        at me, scratch his claws across my body, but he will be like wind,
the same damp air he was when I was eleven and unaware yet

of my big shocking ears stuck out and every day
        let my mother tuck my hair behind them before school. I loved her
fingers against me on those ticklish curls of skin. Yes,

Time is limp today, an old, worn puma. I choose an artichoke. If I am
        eleven again, my ears proud and grand, then I am also six, the body,
even sweeter than my mother's, not dangerous. The man who asks

to see my panties has fallen into a hole. Nothing holds him
        and his pale green hands melt to tufts of asparagus as I peel back
a husk to see the rows of corn, swing my grocery basket

against my leg, feeling nothing for the many people
        this day does not love. Sly, randy, sun-moaning—my day
uses present tense, whispers *Beautiful, beautiful*

all over me. It is good to have my ears. I know
        because I bend to the eggplant. I bend
and listen for her heartbeat.

Aquarium

Whose body is whose, I wondered
    once, last night, late, when we were tangled
as kelp, how it grows without knowing it
    does, every which way, warm, sinewy, plaited
by the currents,

I wondered the *hows* we could grow into
    each other if we did: with no sun to climb to
but the cadence of our bodies, we have raked
    the penniless fountain of propriety, we follow
the moon into the dark, push hair from our faces,
    give shiatsu, crush under, wash each other with the liquids
of God, let go the small noises that parade

as if we are pained, as if too many times
    we did not let our voices slide down, slide up,
as if we could, this time, swim ourselves together, one
    body of muscles and kindly spate, the other of fins
and phenomenon, both no longer inhabited
    by platelets, but a shaken priest, eyelids half shut, fingers
unable to wrap around the curbs of anything, the streaks

and spills of woe, imagination, our tepid days,
    tumbled to the blue rhombus:

we are as open as the mouths of fish
    rising for an oval of air.

NUDe SeLF-POrTraIT

You think I'm going to mention my breasts.
I know you think I'm going to mention my breasts.

Why not wonder instead the fat of my back—that place
the spine is a valley, rising and rounding to the cushy, slack

tops of my hips. Why not peer over the shoulder
and check out the rolls into which my bra strap tucks, chilly flaps

that sometimes—though it disgusts me, too—sport a pimple.
If this does not satisfy you, you might be interested

in my front fat, that sweet pouch of button and gut.
I can make for you a "donut" by squeezing in the extra skin

around my navel. I can offer you not one, not two, but three
waves of chub like grand brushstrokes which make the sea

a roiling bluster on flat canvas. There is nothing so prodigious
as a woman's blundering skin, her torrent of resolutions,

her stolid disregard and self-love, despite hair on her neck,
too-blue veins, an uneven nipple, and there you have it,

that mention of the breasts you have been waiting for, yourself
perhaps a pertinent body of water, blood, bile, stains,

your own delusions of nudity notwithstanding, guessing *someone*
would find you pleasing, the turn of your ear, the soft slap

one knee makes against the other, the uneven scar just above
the pubis. No wonder the Chinese word for *fat* is "pang,"

pronounced "puhng," but landing like a pinch, like a bird dropping
on the warped deck of a ship tossing and sacred on your only sea.

EXPIATION

For those who follow me cozily out the door, for the one
so close in line last night I felt his hard-on, the ones

who say *hello,* looking at the breasts, *how are you,*
the puffy-lipped polo shirt wearers who discuss my

classes on days my skirts are thigh-high and my legs
must be making a sound only they can hear,

for those who say God is not even one-quarter She,

for the pokes at ribs and claps on the *ass* given with
a smile, the knuckles against the neck when I'm pulling

at the doorhandle, the heavy beerish pocket of a mouth,
the pinches while asking what my shirt says, *sweet thang,*

for the white vans whose drivers honk *honkhonk,*
the doorbells I cannot answer because it could or could not

or could or could not be just Jehovah's Witness men,
the poorly lit parking lots reminding me they found

drops of Trisha's urine behind the swimming pool but
never found Trisha, for the *hot damns* pelted out rolled-down

windows, the Spanish they don't think I understand one aisle over,

the middle-aged men pushing their children in carts and taking full
bodied looks in the frozen food section, the trucker on I-65,

the condom on his fingers pointing at me,

for the dialogue of cottage cheese thighs, the raw popping
laughs when virgins walk by or

butch girls or acned girls or flat girls,
the jokes about bumpy nipples packed-tuna pussy the ugliest

fucks you'd ever seen can't buh
lieve they lettem live that ugly,

for them you do a service, quiet-hearted man, your
fingers on my forehead, your face like rain,

landing anywhere, something clean of your eyes
when you say *fair one,* when you listen to me,

and for them you oil the humbling of age, you redeem
mankind, you hold out the pearl you found in your chest,

the one each man has, and it speaks to the softest,
scaredest part of me, the part naked and artless

as a woman's open body, for all of them you
make me think I could unravel into the imperfect,

the sweat, the gingered cadence
of humanity with one of you.

LOST In THe CanT

I like it when you're on top, he said. *It means
you want it.* He was right: on top, I could

see that spot between the urbane coins
of his nipples, that small, hallowed dip where

breastplates meet, south of the clavicle, I could almost
touch it. I wanted to unwrap the place, reach into him

like a woman reaches into a bowl,
like a man reaches into a woman.

I would find intercostal straw-sized holes,
bare pupils, black like my father's, many and many

of them, riposte for his oblique kisses, the blank
spaces that never got filled. All the tacit arches

of blood, there. I would understand then, how bodies work
against each other, comically black and blue, the seiche rising,

me, thrown by the nexus, him, lost in the cant. Those countries
between us might sing: great, recovered skin; wet

and pleasant cylinders; pulse of heart,
she denies fissure now, *on top,*

the way she used to finger petals stripped from the rose,
her thumbprint curling to its perfect red spoon.

krash

Too many things happen quickly. Like the bullet
shot into a mattress. Like this morning, the diligent rhythm

of the porch swing, a finch with her breakfast among the mulch
and roots, and I didn't think the *Thud* I heard was a car crash

because the word *thud* was too slow. There wasn't even
the fantastic *Krash!* you hear in movies. It might not

have happened at all, but then a man and a woman stood
on the street, peering at footprint-sized dents and a little

steam. They squinted, exchanged cards as you would
cheap gifts, embarrassed and slippery. So little time was wasted

even the sunshine was not flustered, though I thought things would slow,
time would thicken into some painful pudding around the bodies,

reducing the speed of eyelashes, glances, arching wrists
and elbows. Instead, it was: *I slept with her.* As quick as the final

stage of birth, the way the pushing and moans slicken
into an immediate red life, your words bulked enough to allow

that weightlessness of confession, but your tongue lay, far more inert
than a tongue should be in such moments, for if anything dispenses time

shouldn't it be the tongue, the twisting wet muscle that will form words
days and weeks later, words to take the sting out, like *bamboozle,*

a wonderful deceleration for the mouth: our fingers meshed
in the carpet, our faces down, speaking into air that snaps

and syrups, speaking, and each syllable falling
calmly as thirty shekels into your hands.

Prose, I say, Plasma

The night we both do not sleep, I tell you, *The body is an overturned pail
of bees.* And you say, *The body is a patch of caraway.* The chickpeas soak,
the recipe for hummus waiting as most wait, on a countertop, like careful

news. In the morning you find a purple onion, an avocado, *Cartesian,* you say,
the quartered remains of a tomato and we eat all things eversible and holy
in the form of an omelet. Food: the only entr'acte for us, isn't that the way

of it? The body, the bees, each demiurgical kick enough to sweeten
our hapless honey-lack. *Prose, I say, Plasma. Give me something endogenous,*
and all you can do is tend those precious sounds: Andrés Segovia,

the bucket on the ground almost angry with onomatopoeia, what
you will still call, years from now, my rigamarole—beauty—among
the calla lilies, every spade the obscurant and rightly so, my love.

Here it is afternoon, and we have just begun to haunt our ideas
of each other, saunter by, the bodies we trade in every now and again
for talk, for appetites, for window-view. Here we glee in paronomasia,

our forms of humor slowly colliding until the wide sun settles down,
each limb a given axis, more to do with tongues than speech. But say
the lentils, celery, carrots, minced garlic, cilantro, say they speak

calumny, it is here in the valiant stalk of your body, the tender
petals, *Unmeasured ingredients, give me anything Aeolian.* Darling: soon
we will be able to sleep, we will pour olive oil into the sea.

InsIDe a THIn EGG

The man next door is calmly standing over
　　his two dogs saying, "No Barking, No Barking,"
carrying the vowel of the *No* out like a one-note

song. I learned the song as I slept, the same time
　　my husband's cat dragged in a baby robin, stripped
of feathers, the wood floor dappled in reds. It took

a great, hollow time—as if inside an old rubber
　　ball—to hear myself singing the word, the one long
note. I covered the bird and stopped, rubbing my fingers

together in the air, as if the corners of the house held
　　another answer. I scooped and dropped her
into the trash bin. In the shower I scrubbed myself tender. Now

I sit, watching the stupid cat sniff the floor where I wiped
　　each staccato drop clean. My appetite is gone—
not from the fluids or torn body, how the lavender skin

of the robin's eyelids wrinkled, her shape
　　drooping into the curve of my hand—
but because it occurs to me, calm as it is,

how vicious our domestic creatures are,
　　all the desperate noises they must make:
to be scolded, to be extolled, to be known

at all. Is it the lambent tune of humanity—the one word,
　　the one-noted *No*—which separates us from animals?
In the bed where we made love last night, I open

the dictionary. Six entries for the word
　　no. It discourages me, the vague, disparate, common
way this word works on the page. I let go

the thick binding, the letters on half-moons
    falling forward, *M-N, K-L, I-J,* I lay my palm
on the tight, round shoulder of my husband,

not awake but moving toward me, exhaling
    a dream through his nostrils. I will not look
at his eyelids, lavender veins running subtly across

his temples. Here is an upside-down-boy
    next to the word *headstand,* here the profiles
of Adolf Hitler and Alfred Hitchcock on the same page,

here hydrangea and Aldous Huxley one column
    apart. My eyes close. Inside a thin egg,
I move until my mouth is on my husband's shoulder.

BUCKETFUL OF RADIANT TOYS

(Tautology in the Presence of A. R. Ammons)

It's a question like, Where does the money go?
Mango-Cinnamon Tea, sliced cheese, a matinee:
orthopedic running shoes, leaky compressor,
an Ethiopian girl *Derartu Motuma* who brings

water from the well and likes Math best. It's
a question like, Are we *earth things?* Water in our veins,
appreciation for squirrels outside the window, sex,
the occasional asperity, the hairless spot on a man's

thighs. It's not so much the question as the curio, Whom
do you trust? Wedding pictures, blood draws,
ziti boiling on the stove, neighbors, batteries
in the fire alarm. What it might be "like"

is that there are no questions, not in the mind,
not in the ground we are driven into, the indifferent
sunsets, the *bucketful of radiant toys.* There are smears
in appellation: I would tell you this man I'm in love with

is effulgent, I would say nothing around us will wait,
even the morning dares us to speak, raspy, small voices,
of our dreams. Only everything he says, and I say,
works the polarities of allowance: and now

I know: we will go or we won't. It will last or—but there, see?
I have done it again. Every phrase will be this, *The Unifying Principle,*
ancient and rather incapacitated to know origins, radiance, even
the small virtues of economy and bunk. This man I'm in love with,

he is the balloon I let *aloose.* It's a question like, When you die,
do the colons still breathe, do the dots work as doors, bulbs,
letter openers? The resolution, sir, is in your hands, folded over
you now, only the arch of your thumb is a question.

supernova love shah

She is a thousand pieces, scraped together. Debutantes,
all. *This holy water.* His arms, each like men

themselves, bustling under the whole skin
of the arms, strong solid men, she wants to pull them

together, dry skin, dry dark skin, arms like men. Skin,
the word, so close to sin, take the one letter. Take it

out. So she is *overcome:* three definitions: Mint-heavy,
hoary breath. Shoulder, tight round shoulder. Music.

Ety. < It doesn't say, it doesn't say. But she remembers
this place, where she cannot touch, but be touched,

every shining time, amenable, unable, scraped into a thousand
ugly pieces. A thousand, she thinks, a bit much: orotund, melanoid,

palpatory, paraffinic, fissile, yes, dactylic, vis-à-vis, supernovae
—and 991 more—not all of them ugly. Some say it is *beautiful drowning,*

This holy water. She says, Please, from beneath the eyelids, just this once,
don't mock. Don't dangle him, God. So she is *overcome:* The man. Me,

the woman. Orphic, all. And here it whips like November
into them. *Ety.* < Fr. *paysan* < OFr. *paisant,* peasant.

See PEASANT. Oh, but blessed are the poor in spirit, God,
blessed are the peasants. Precious lost, precious found. She has waited

so long—it doesn't work that way, I know, I know. His arms stretch,
two men in salutation. And they, the paisanos, paddle into *This holy water,*

separately, one gratis, one scraping, and singing plaintive songs,
of the love Shah, of the over come: fetal, black *beautiful drowning,*

arthritic spine of the dictionary, him, her, the kernel, the tedium,
whatever we are. Now osculant. Now alone.

sprezzatura

To his book's end this last line he'd have placed: Jocund his muse was,
but his life was chaste. —Robert Herrick, "To His Book's End"

Here you are in an airport terminal, plastic rows
    of empty seats, when a man sits down
exactly next to you, his forearm brushing your shoulder
    in relocation, the musk-red smell of him

rising and settling on the fine hairs of your upper lip.
    It has begun, subtly. You are slightly incensed,
the effrontery to notice you, sit close to your body
    in this place of transit, this fluorescent tube

of comings-and-goings. You cannot look at him,
    but you know he is beautiful. It works
your chariness. The man doesn't speak to you, doesn't stir
    in your direction: he is busy in his laptop,

cuffs starchly encountering the keyboard. So,
    after a moment, you go back to reading
Hesperides and *Noble Numbers,* alternatively. He
    is probably off to St. Louis, and you,

to San Diego. Nevertheless, it has affected the diagonals
    of your face, the place you are *woman,*
and it has become important for him to notice your
    good posture, the moist inner elbow, the freckled top

of your hand. He must do nothing. Arrivals and departures
    crackle over your head, the fanned, stale air
rustles your consideration of *cleanly wantonness, wild civility.*
    All of this, a small everything, confuses an unknown

dialogue in you: like the chinchilla, raised for its soft, pale coat,
    then taken from the cage to be the pet
of a gentle Argentine. So this moment, *gathering rosebuds,*
    the gratuitous and the solemn, wandering between

Scylla and Charybdis. And here, finally, you know why
    Robert Herrick separated his joie de vivre
from his foreskin offering to Christ, his "Upon the Nipples
    of Julia's Breast" from "To His Conscience"—

why he bound them all in *one fat little octavo volume:*
    nothing ends. No, nothing will end.

I INSPECT MY FACE

Sometimes after I am done
crying, dried up as a breast of milk,
I will make myself cry again,
just to watch how it works,
the cheeks pulling closer
to the ears for comfort, the chin
growing a hundred years old.
I think of my mother, when she will live
without my father and his
grown-soft ways, or the woman
and her baby smashed under a school bus
by a sleepy truck driver. Mostly, though,
I think about myself, the tumors lurking
in my nodes, or the men I have loved
tossing me aside. The best part: spill.
My blue-iris-eyes alone with color,
clear wet nubs rising to drop perfectly
over the rim and develop their slow,
pleasing fall. In these moments,
I love myself. I know nothing
else to comfort my body but my
body. It helps to turn the face
and examine acne: that one
spot reddened with trouble,
my fingers smoothing over
small valleys and knolls, waiting
like the rest of my skin
for something to happen.

negligee, negligent, negligence

Here, sidling up to the house where she was raised, the rooms aglow with ghosts,
daytime ghosts in cahoots with the sunshine, panes unable to hold a single thing
back: her father, squinting at a verse, her mother, licking stamps.

Nothing here was a waste of time.
Nothing crept so slowly.

Here, the slender neck of Nefertiti rises in limestone from the photographs,
  All this fiddle, the ears begin to say,
  Beyond, the eyebrows say,
  Nothing nefarious, from the slender shoulders, *as your own heart.*

What in history would you call your own?

She curls against the brick as best she can, the simple girl,
giving her body to the hard wall of memory, the topography of this place
home: once she saw a peregrine falcon, heard a hundred pond frogs.

And wouldn't you know a girl is only a scrap of soft fabric with legs,
  walking backwards toward love,
  strolling sideways toward love,
  fluttering across the waters in her way.

She turns. For all your permanent shimmer, the cloth of my skin
is young, is questing, dilapidated with chance.
Something, O Queen, knows me better than I know myself.

God shaped the fields of sorghum just so?

JUST WANTED TO SHOW YOU A PICTURE OF MYSELF

Here is your face ready for the two years in Turkey—
bad coffee, stealing cigarettes from lieutenants—then orders
and helicopters and a bullet in the hip outside Hanoi
during the four tours you don't quite talk about
or the things in your face (which now I see weren't there
before the wet the red the jungle) before the which the between
the denouement things in your face with your hands
around my throat once you called me a whore just look at you
take something particular the skin on the neck the collar the tie
the insignia on every button I can't remember if it was the Army
or Navy or Marines it would kill you me not remembering but

here is your face cheekbones I did not inherit
from a great great great Sioux grandmother and teeth
so familiar—you look almost settled into
your skin—tight across the jaw spartan over rims of lips
that grin just look at you the strata of eyes and brows and brim
of that stiff official hat really you are heady in the eyes
as if in 28 months there will not be an M16 put
in your hands to help you rout someone before he
routs you the tea-colored men women children
you have seen it is not in the eyes back then
just a Sir Yes Sir, Helluva good time Sir—and cleanly, too—

I'm not sure I am a glimmer there no matter how
that saying enlists itself in my ego I know there have been
bodies slack crimson puddled by your trigger bodies
alive writhing with yours bodies bodies slumped out naked
from her bowl of your investment (which concede your second life)—
I would like to know you in the first—put my fingers in your ears
like I used to and draw with markers on your back
call you Hot Riler and be small like an animal against you
before these things before the blonde went black
went gray in a one by one amendment of the hairs
the country called a heart jolting at night when I trip on the stairs

It's me Just me and this face a version of the other
face so close to mine your breath is a body sometimes
saying things like Bullshit you don't fuck around and
I was 18 when this was taken

II

Jagged with Love

IT'S THE FIRST THING

They teach you in lifeguard courses:
a person will take you down, though you
are trying to help, a person will hurt you,
he will drown you, despite himself.
This is what panic will do, even to the most
sane, its sharp strings under every last
fingernail and pulled taut by circumstance,
say, a sandbar you didn't know would drop
out or a wave from nowhere, panic will yank
its cords, will make you dance its terrible jig,
and when someone, even a strapping someone,
comes to help, panic begins its buoyant song,
gumming your reason, and even if you
have been the gentlest soul, swerving to miss
raccoons on the road and bending
to kiss the paraplegic women in a home,
you will scratch and latch and grasp
that someone with a fervor you could almost taste,
tangy and succinct, like a fine mustard, firm
with the gut of its tiny seed, golden as the sun's gut,
ferment of a season you anticipate, one
you have yet to know, one you must
and have yet to know.

MY FATHER, NAKED AT 28

My grandmother is spread over Yucca Valley,
out past Joshua Tree where my father dropped
acid till he was 28. He was not invited
to trek up the mile and a half of semi-arid
underbrush, where the path wound like a dirty thread
through redwoods, where my uncles and grandfather
each took a handful of her, sprinkled her over
the Saradine Cliffs and said a prayer. They told the air
things like *Mother, you are home.* They wiped their faces
with white cuffs and rubbed ash-covered hands over
flesh-dry ones, and drove home, and told
my father where she was spread, sent him the program
with pictures of lilies and portions of hymns.

Today my father takes me out to the tip
of the porch, faces west, as if he is not nine states
from her ashes. *She wrestles Forgivers of the air
now. The air and not the earth.* He points to where the sun
mellows and pinks the sky like raspberry sherbet my mother
serves. My father says, *I've called her Helen since
I was 17. My brothers told her I never loved her.*

I was 11 when I saw the picture of my father: bathrobe open,
genitals covered with a glued-on shred of paper, his beard a set
of wiry brown wafers stretched to his chest, his
eyes like half-cracked eggs, blue yolks of bitter
intelligence. Grandmother had said to me, *That's
your dad long-long ago, before he got saved. I like
to remind myself how far he's come.*

OLD COUNTRY woman

And what do you think you'll know by the end of it, her wrists as soft as plums,
her whole white head lit by God, her funny phrases sticking to you.

Instead of *no* she'd say *leave it be,* which makes no sense whatsoever,
which makes the least sense of anything she said, which you find yourself

murmuring over the furled edges of your husband's face, his aching
love, over the bodies of your children who scramble in and out of the tub,

wet and brilliant with laughter, their plastic toys sunk and sunk again.

Leave it be, she'd say. Especially once: the scrappy jay in her pear tree
and your brother's BB gun cocked and your brother saying sweetly, *Go on. Go on.*

She is far from you, as far as the word *old* and the word *no* and only on days
like today—when a man kisses you and you must work to keep your mouth

from turning into a thousand birds and the two daughters you have made together
are asleep and not a single person in the world asks your name—

calling her an old country woman is only the beginning of the moments
you will have, Mondays when he takes the girls to visit his mother,

in St. Clair where the starlings *fly sky-pepper,* year-round, when you scrub lime stains
from the shower wall, spoon out macaroni, answer *I reckon* in a conference call.

What do you know by the end of it except that you hate for him to hunt quail
and if you remember in October you show the girls how to make necklaces

from pumpkin seeds and once when it was completely still, your hands
sachets for the black air, you turned into an old country woman, you knew

exactly what it was to be dead and you fell from the sky.

He Talks Again of California

My father tells me tonight of eucalyptus honey,
how he'd lugged buckets
    of it at five years old, maybe four.
The orange groves, he says, were
        flanked by eucalyptus trees—they
      broke the Santa Ana wind

and held in the heat of the smudge-pots,
which burned to keep frost
    from the orange blossoms.
That was before the wind mills, he says,
        before California sucked every last wisp
      of energy from the wind with mills

on each corner, splicing the sunsets
and adding a funny, mechanical touch
    to the view from Hadley's, the best for date shakes.
Not shakes on dates, he says, but actual date
        shakes; made from dates in the grove like
      oranges in the grove, dates that grew

as grapes in a bunch, laid out
to wrinkle and crystallize with sugar,
    dates, he says, sweeter than your mom.
He doesn't say, Those were the days.
        He doesn't say, You can't get eucalyptus honey
      anywhere anymore, not even San Jose.

He doesn't say, I'll make you a date shake
someday. He says nothing more.
    After dinner he leans against the sink, holds himself still.
He stands with his plate in his hand, and I watch him fade,
        looking out the window
      into the dark gut of Ohio.

JAGGED WITH LOVE

The year my father stopped yelling, I began
    to see a counselor. I cried to her, all the buds
        of forgiveness stubborn as flax, the color
    of a forgotten wall, having burrowed

for years, and now with the coaxing
    of this woman, psalmist's verse, dry-erase board,
        I wept stupidly, like a girl
    who's torn the head from her doll, meaning to.

My nightmares recurred. I stopped sleeping,
    stopped eating meals, only the forkfuls I could muster
        while my roommates gawked. I stayed days in my room
    and found music that cried with me, for pity's sake,

the blue stomachache of life, life shorn up as a skull.
    My counselor kept mentioning
        the *mortal coil*, and here I was, she said, somewhere
    between Eeyore and catatonia. How's your sex drive, she'd ask, and,
The centipede in your dreams still speaks?

One day a sign outside her office building says, *Watch
    for falling tar.* We start in on the fainting spells,
        the one and only slap, the first time he called me a whore. Men
    on the roof keep throwing over bags of powder, their tools,

their helmets flag past the window and hit the ground
    like a knee-jerk memory: his breath
        blowing out *Shit For Brains.* His soldier's stance,
    close enough to my face for a kiss, or a small,

calculated bite. Last night, I start, I finally dreamed of Vietnam.
    Good, she says, and marks it down, Good. No, I say, it was me,
        giving birth in the jungle. My father was nowhere, not with a gun,
    not hunting Charlie. My father, I say, was not even dead.

And then, as sometimes happens, my hour is up, and I am
    standing outside. It smells burnt. I look up, watching for tar to fall,
        but even that, I don't know what it means: how do you
        watch for something to fall? Just walk, I guess, and this

is what I do, chin tipped to the sky, thrumming with the urge
    to love complexity, as I know it, jagged with love.

OUT SMARTING

It started with the slice of pumpkin pie
    you warmed up at breakfast. When
you burned your tongue on the first bite, something

    inside you slipped like a button into the Something
else, a little choking. You didn't know who to be angry at,
    yourself or the hot orange flesh of the pie, and inside

your mouth the burned spot scratches like your father's
    chin. While walking to work,
the tambourine sky fell on you in notes

    and it almost felt good, denim sticking
to your thighs, a drip resting in the cave of your ear. When
    you tilted your head to let it roll, another drop

dropped straight into your eye. Straight in, as if all along
    your eye has not been an eye but concentric circles and
Something finally hit its target. At work, when

    you wrote a letter to an old friend (you were supposed to be
editing Jack Bucco's dissertation), the button tightened. Words
    would not bless the page, clumsy and large as they are sometimes,

and carping, like your aunts badgering each other
    during the holidays, words not really words but overweight
feelings, unhoneyed, uncaptured, unhonest. Mid-afternoon

    the man you're dating, the kind-of kind of dating,
phoned with a sweet, sexy *hello,* and the button rippled,
    and next he told you his ex-girlfriend is back

in town and he'd like you to meet her, maybe you could all go
    for dinner. Dinner and a movie—nothing fancy. After work
you run on the indoor track at Ruddy's, letting your body go

raw, go hard around the corners. When you hear
a man with dyed blue hair say to his friend, "—but then
    I'd have to go be a doctor, and I don't want to

do that—" your Something folds over and over and into your
    brother in med school, who called last week, roughly sobbing
because he failed the kinesthesiology exam, your

    brother who never cries, who never calls, who is
the smartest person you know, who *does* want to do that. When
    you turn lap 34 (8 more for a 10K), you

realize why you are running. There are too many buttons, their
    X-ing threads wet and tight as tentacles, and you'd like to think
these small, rust-red chips are doing something dramatic inside,

    colliding, or screaming, or writhing, or melting. But they aren't.
They are fastening the Somethings together, like a dense wool sweater
    around the heart, and your tongue is scratching

the pink-pebbled roof of your mouth and the rain is bulleting the gym
    windows and people all over the world are arching
their fingers into the air, under pages of text, into wads of hair, around

    the girth of a phone. Your legs go, your left lung is ragged, you
are chanting, and though it comes out *lap 41 41 41,* what you
    are actually saying is *I can hurt myself more than you can.*

LAST APRIL

Tonight your father tells you one of his fifth graders
    is a rapist. The boy took his cousin out to the garage last April,
but since they're family, since nobody in Indiana wants to read
    about a boy raping a boy, nothing has ever been done: no police file,
no juvey hall. It's a punishment of its own in Indiana: secrets
    aren't secrets for long. But what, we forget to ask, could we find
under the linoleum of our hearts? Nothing of grammar, logic,
    or rhetoric, a triple way, as it were, to eloquence.

Each day your father encounters the small bodies of children,
    their broken toys like their minds and their eager choices: which
and who and how many. Each day our small bodies grow longer
    and thicker and muddier. They institutionalized Jared,
the raped second grader, up in White River. At E. O. Muncie Elementary,
    a teacher's assistant has been assigned to watch his cousin Tyler
at breakfast, at recess, on his way to the school bus. *He still*
    trips the fat kids, my dad says. *He told everyone today he had beer*
in his backpack. We sit in the noiseless room, our chins ruefully
    tucked, the game of Trivial Pursuit now abstruse, a mile from our fingers.

Tonight it began with the phone call, you excusing yourself
    from the volley of gaudy factoids to talk to the Tallahassee
Police Department. *We'd like to ask you a few questions about the previous owner*
    of your house, a gruff woman started. *We'd like to know*
if you've spoken recently with John Trent. No, you tell her, and you peek
    your head into the living room, working to catch
your mother's question: Which U.S. President died with 317 slaves and 150 acres?
    You're thinking, George Washington!–You're thinking, and he freed
them all in his will! You are happy about this, the first abolitionist.
    The woman is saying, *So you haven't spoken with him, not concerning*

the house, not at all? No, you say again, baffled by the inquiry, scanning
      your mind for details of the man you'd met only once, John Trent,
sweating in the September heat, his prosthetic leg squeaking,
      his two-year-old calm as a potted plant on the carpet that smelled
of canines and tired cigarettes. *I didn't interact with him, really,* you say,
      my realtor did, and, *if I may ask, what's this in regards to?* You
are suddenly solemn and fatigued, seconds away from defensive,
      having arrived yesterday in Indiana to visit your family,
to leave all of Florida behind for at least a week, and here's this sergeant,
      wanting to *ask you some questions* like a forkful of slowly wound
noodles. *Ma'am,* she says, *John Trent is a sex offender.* She pauses.

We've got a warrant for his arrest and we're looking for leads
      to his whereabouts. Another, longer pause, almost a silence.
Ma'am? Ma'am, please, a date, a dialogue, anything. Finally
      you fumble, *Oh, sure, sure,* but you are having trouble
recalling his face, only his sweat-curled bangs will come into focus
      and a flashlight you found in the closet next to a box

of unused checks. What you can barely register as thinking is *I wasn't*
      expecting this. Two minutes ago you'd been answering questions
with *Yogi Berra* and *Robert Kennedy.* Then again, who is ever expecting
      the bulk of a man's body, his elbows or his eyes,
both variously thrown, to re-enter the house of the mind. *And I sleep*
      in his room. And I shower in his shower. It's not *thinking*
so much as an imagining, those shadows you cannot help. That's right:
      the mind cannot help, the mind cannot take the words apart. It begs
which, who, how many. Those carpets are gone, the walls painted,
      the counters resurfaced. You cannot know what *sex offender* means.

Back at the board game, your brother has rolled
      a four, he counts out the spaces with his pinkie finger and your sister
pulls out a card to ask him *green:* What popular vegetable was originally
      cultivated from the bitter stalk of sleepage? Your mother leans
toward your dad, making their guesses behind cupped hands
      and even though you are vegetarian you cannot think
straight: stalk, root, herb; chives, radish, sage. There are other ways,
      ways the heart has to tear itself out. You had forgotten
you actually own a *home,* that place with doors and eaves, rooms
      and bulbs. Nothing skulked. Nothing shimmied.

Your brother fingers his newly grown beard and gnaws
    on the stick pretzel he has been pretending to bogart. *Celery,*
he enunciates, and your parents erupt with approval, your sister nods
    and reaches for a small green wedge to place in the pie,
pleased. You are trying not to be dramatic, slumped in your chair,
    but you begin by saying, *You'll never guess who that was,* and your voice
sounds rumpled, far away, like the flush of a toilet in a distant room.

CHRISTMAS, 2000

My father has a pocket full of things even he does not know. In the morning
　　with his cup, snow outside the window and his church across
　　　　the way, the early hours have called him *man* at their first birr of light,
sent from the sun with a name. This Christmas, nothing is wrong: my brother
　　has not dyed his hair, my sister passed her boards, I am not in love
with a black man. This Christmas I notice how my uncles close him
　　out of conversation like a musty room, effectually sending him
to the couch with Uncle Jim, who is on his way to, if not already,

drunk, and who is most interesting of them all, watching football from inside
　　a featherless mind. My uncles say, *Alfalfa? Hayseed?* On the sides
　　　　of his eyes, my father's skin droops into Greek letters. This is the year—
I should have guessed even then, in the quick clasp of holiday—my father
　　will call forth my sympathy, small, consistent buckets carried in
from the shore of adolescence, where he banned me,
　　　　where I crawled in the foam of his crashed voice, his pulling
fury. We do not, probably we will never, talk about the day

I found his hands around my throat, not squeezing—not squeezing
　　at all—but holding, perhaps for the sake of what he did not know
　　　　how to wield, perhaps in the sheer, ensconced loss of control,
his cloak of red-white-&-blue so soiled and so electrifying. Though I do not know it yet,
　　this is the year I will cry for my father in a wet stratagem: knowledge,
　　distance, despair. At first this is despite myself, my fear of him
　　　　unable to sour into a wholesome hate, easing instead
into an uncertainty, a loss spilling over, his own wounds

wounding me: in the caverns of his mouth they say, *I do not know*
　　if my father loved me; in his bones, the venom of circumstance; in every thing,
　　　　everything, Vietnam. This is how it began, my body on the floor,
reckless, yelling out his terrible, forgiven name to God. No—this is how
　　it began: there, on the couch with Jim, head thrown back, lips
　　slightly open, fallen asleep, his face stepped back from its sturdy
　　　　pulpit. The bad dream he is having furrows his skin, tells how
his old, rapacious core is susceptible to horror and rush,

the helplessness of a dream, the dark temper, perhaps, turned on him,
    heavying his heavy pocket. My father stopped being strong.
        This is the year I learn that fear runs, in fact, on legs
of love, but it will be months before I breathe a prayer to topple
        its velocity. It is only Christmas, and we have gathered
    in one room, the periodicity of gifts packing us tight
to each other's bodies, laughing, coughing. Families—these units of purpose,

cannot, even when there is nothing else, learn the language of stillness.
    My father is awake, picking something from his ear. I have my hands
        in my pockets, the surest place for my fingers. Grandmother
and the Christmas tree sit in opposite corners of the enlivened room, keeping
        the world so coolly in a kind of balance. Here is what we are,
    here is what we wish to be: perched inside the ruby ornament, given to the sinking
of meringue, trusting as the towhee at the feeder each carefully pecked winter morning.

LOVE'S BALSA WOOD TRICERATOPS

If there's a place called Here and another called Now,
you must've wandered off from one, bounced off the other,
and never looked back. But I'm figuring it'll be for you

same as a frog's tongue, slung out sticky pink and snapped back
with a little surprise at the end. As you might guess, I'm counting
on something. The kind of break people are always asking for,

praying for a parking spot when all I want is Esther
off dialysis. I'll tell you this, if a girl ever redeemed her dad's
stubborn streak running through her like O negative

it's this one. She says stuff like she's never felt better and Jeepers
Creepers Where'd You Get Them Peepers, now how in the world
does a kid know to say things like that. She told me

you'd be back and I believe her. Me, listening
to my own kid. Yesterday she read me how to put together
this Balsa Wood Triceratops sent over by Father Ken,

and it was almost a joke, the kind of sense it made,
little sticks that build a dinosaur when all you've got to go on
is somebody's idea of order. What it comes to is that it felt

familiar, fiddling with a jumble of pieces, separating *dorsal*
from *torso* when if you haven't been told recently
you can't recall what either means. When we folded up

that little sheet of directions I thought of you,
who'd have kept at it, glue all over your fingers, a match
in your mouth for good luck. In the end, it's this I think

will bring you home. The Here, the Now, how one of them
will do you right, and one wrong, how we'll know
where to go from there, won't we.

KULIBONGBONG FOR LYDIA

My sister   having passed her boards last week   having just lost
the partial cap of her front tooth   chipped on the front steps when she was nine
and running to tell us of *kulibongbongs* on the back wall of our house
   in the Philippines   *kulibongbongs* being *butterflies*
by the warbled news of youth   flown in after the rainy season
delighting   my sister   her body flung
   with happiness on the front steps

now is a doctor   stones burning in her hands   her face
   having taken on a smallness   after fifteen good years
years I spent fractioning holiness   weaving *malcriada*   I tell you
the jagged square of darkness trapped in her smile   says
   unknown woman   soft-footed deer
convivial ricebowl of a woman—   the slight whistle of fricatives
the weight of a trinket against a finger
   the absence of a piece of a tooth lost long   long ago

Is it wrong of me   Lydia   every one of your unassailable sounds
   not yet specified to you as song   to wonder what *kulibongbongs* wait
your corn-tassle body flung   finally   on which man?   your winds
having reached no edge   with me bedlammed little sister
   who stabbed a pencil into the flesh of your palm   only
partially an accident   both of us   churning in horror at your great
sweet blood   graphite-black   Isn't it only wrong to consider   what he will take
   your tooth already claimed   your heart already a horse

III

A RUSH OF BEES

in indiana

It's a surprise to sit outside   this time of November
so comfortably   on the swing with a crash of sun against
your neck   wanting to wear that white dress   only meant
            for indeed   summer   the one you have taken in a man with

what you thought opaque white   not quite so   or so
he told you   after he'd swept a finger across your cheek
            when you said   Saul   I don't know   if we deserve this
and he said   close your eyes   and think about it

What he meant was   don't think   What he meant was   let me kiss you
            Sitting outside with a spot of flowers huddled   against the fence
you are glad   it still feels like summer   your mother has used the word
unseasonable to describe it   though you would have said anomalous

        anything else sounds giddy   and these are solemn   days
with the coming of winter   still coming   only pitched a length from our minds
            You let him kiss you of course   and you're thinking *of course*
because this is the man   who put a spin on you   who took
        and took from you   all of it starting with that white dress
that day in the park   after church   he must have   watched the shadows

the light across your body   to tell you   later he knew
exactly what kind of panties you wore   tugging the slight
            white strap   at your hip   all you could think to say was
wait   to which he said   sorry   sorry   sorry

what you meant was   no
what he meant was   let me try again   in five   four   three
            A tree frog starts a slow crawl across the seat   of the swing   you have
never seen a frog crawl as if a spider   one limb at a time   each wet nub reaching

        carefully you   reach to touch   the frog   so small
so composed   and unaware   you mean not to hurt it   just
reassure yourself   of living   you too have been that still
a thin line   of sweat on the crest   of your lip

LIKE THE NUDES OF LUCIAN FREUD

Consider that sounds—*leg, capsule, kickshaw, no, evanescent,*
enough, raspberry, water, novella—matter: the woman dying

of stomach cancer in Los Angeles speaks to her granddaughter
in Indianapolis, speaks around heavy massaging in her head

and the many years. It is not what the woman says to the girl
or what the girl says to the woman: it is how. The mouth

as egress means the mouth as auspice. These movements of the mouth,
ripe circles of air passing out our bodies, air from the very galaxies

of God, those solar systems of length and volume, pitch
and crest: words come from here. Don't we like to think they begin

in the mind, crawling pleasantly to the tongue on knees
of necessity. Perhaps, and the girl pulls her body in like a fetus

around the phone, she looks at the brown angles of her legs
and the *Chronicles of Narnia* on the shelf. Words here

encyst: *How are you doing* and *Well what have you been up* to spin
so easily, away from the blood, the passage of fluids

to and fro. They soak in a near-empty tub. There is a moment
when she wonders what the mouth is for. She remembers cantaloupe,

her grandmother's manicured nails, a knife slipping
and the first time she ever heard a woman say *damn.* The girl

must make something in her mouth, *hurry,* and give it over
to the phone. *If I were a snap away If I had come to see you*

long ago. And it is diachronic: the journey of this small lexicon,
the slippery face. For years she will not know it was *cui bono,*

too much that fell through her mouth of the anxious, existing
world, like the nude portraits of Lucian Freud: open woman,

hard gray-blues on her skin, each switch from sable to hog brush
applying *representational realism.* In Los Angeles, the woman

gathers herself, says something terrible like *If you were only
as close as the corner, honey, Grandma would come running she would*

rip off these tubes and come running. Yes, years later she decides
the mouth is for listening. Auscultation, even dumbly. It was

the fathomless sound of *goodbye,* two syllables: the space of a button,
breaking an orange from the branch, the tapping down of a nail.

DaUGHTer In THe
waiTInG ROOm

They will lift your hair to the roots and buzz close
    to the scalp, they will brush away the brown
        with the gray from your shoulders and you will watch
    it all lie still on the floor and slippered feet will step lightly

on it. They will make lines on your skin with surgery marker
    that is the same dark purple as under your eyes,
        they will put numbers and large words on your
    chart, knowing you will not see them, knowing you

will only understand what bits of encouragements they
    dispense to you in busied inside voices. They tell you
        it is not cancer, they tell you it is a small hole in the skull,
    using golf balls to describe its size. While I am sitting here,

I would like to tell them some things. They should use
    different measurements, never saying *as big as.* They should
        always say *as small as* an apricot, a baby's fist,
    a Mexican Wedding Cake. *As small as* an Oh-ing mouth,

a closed rose, an okey-dokey circle made by thumb
    and pointer finger. They should find some way to let you know
        the absence of something this size is as fixable
    as a foreign presence this size. And they should wait

until you have been wheeled from the room, they should bend
    at the knees and pick up the fallen strings of your hair
        with their own ungloved fingers, they should put
    the browns and grays into a plastic bag, they should take

the same dark purple marker and label the bag *Mother's.*

A RUSH OF BeeS

After you take off your shirt and bra and lie down,
after he spreads the blue jelly under the breast
over your heart, you are still so that your breast
will stay beneath the towel for the first, cold
touch of the instrument and then for each nod of its smooth
metal top, indifferent as a mushroom to the folds of your skin.

Suddenly—there it is, and he says *Ah ha,* and *Here we go,* as if
he has found a dollar bill on your nipple and a trolley stop
in the overlap of your breast. Unamazed, he has
seen the heart before, so he starts in again with the dull
questions neither of you care to attend to, but you answer
anyway and with a patience you do not remember having.

Your voice has become shy within you, introduced,
as it were, to the dignified pulp of your body,
the beautiful fist jumping in oranges and yellows
on the screen, blooming by your personal iambs.
He can see you are watching, he can see you want
to know, so he tells you, and you could swear your ears

grow as huge as the room to handle, to hoist up his heavy syllables
and store them like an oak armoire in a space you will one day
return to: atrioventricular, mitral stenosis, sinoatrial, carditis.
He traces your heartbeat, pulling blues and greens
from its edges, he follows the dips, looking for a "leak"
in the valves, he taps the big round button to record it all.

He tells you it is good to see someone with vitality
after hours and days of geriatrics, their
bodies dismal and hovering like a bad forecast.

After you watch your own heart, you will never again call its work
beating or *pumping.* There are no broad-shouldered men in front
of a fiery door in there, no rusty handles to churn the night long.
You have mistaken rhythm for force. Cadence for exertion.
Now, you see left, right atria, left, right ventricle,
thick petals hung fastidiously over a graceful

rush of bees, one silky jolt giving way to the other,
and there, also, something you cannot see, it must be
what they call the *heart of hearts,* it holds the petals together
from the center—you can't see it but you imagine it is stern,
stunning as the pit in an avocado's soft flesh. This
even the instrument does not know of, does not fathom,

wired to its meters and sensors, clocks and pixels. Your breast
is under a towel, your body a solid wish, and there you are,
your brilliant flower, your dancing bees, lilting, lilting, lilting.

After he has taken the picture away, flipped a switch
and left the room, you wipe the jelly from your body,
you slip on your bra and your shirt. You are aware of a rich,
jagged fiber that ta-TUMS across the tube of your arms,
the half-moons of your nose, the small, hard line of ankle bone.
Now you've seen your own heart working, that repository

of feeling, that seat of love, it is no longer a word or an idea
to be skipped like a stone across conversation: *eat your heart out,
take heart, bless your heart.* No, an entire woman lives there,
a system of stars, a fine, long fall of water, an esplanade of God.

At the front desk, he tells you the results will be in next week and how
startlingly (*That's what it is—*) you remind him of his last girlfriend.
It is hard to know what to say. His remark seems to reach
over you, a cloud of moths nearing your house at the pale end of day,
the day you found your house a home, its doors wavering
open and shut in the wind, its fields the smallest world of pollen.

THe surgery

FOr M.

Today her father shampoos her hair, gently, a blue basin
    on his knees and her head in his hands. Her arms lie
stiff in their deliberate T, never leaving horizontal

with the stitches. Tubes drain blood from left and right
    dorsal side, and occasionally pus seeps down. She
is falling asleep, Mother having brought a clean towel,

the fire still riding on top her ribs. Bearable,
    she thinks, bearable. There is less inside her body.
It was simple: a map on each breast by black marker,

skin, scalpel, gauze, more gauze. There was *reduction,*
    yes: the gene, cheated. Even now, she feels
as though something has been returned to her.

Her father's fingers move easily round the bulb
    of her head. Here, since she is good and flat
on her back for ten to fourteen days, she recalls separately

the boys in junior high, goes through them each
    with the eidetic flourish of a calligraphy pen, settles
on Stace McBremen, loops falling from his stupid name,

his seamless name, his face she remembers with the scar
    above the lip from football, tawny hair, how he said to her
in Home Ec, against the marmoreal cupboards, measuring

spoons lightly in her hand, *You know, you could be a porn star
    with those.* There wasn't space to pull away, to pull back
the puffs of baking soda falling to the floor. She rolls,

almost to a dream, through the girls in junior high, tying
    a burgundy ribbon to the ponytail of appositioned Megan,
Eun Jin, Kirstin, how they eyed her risen skin, told the others

what older sisters had said in excellent secrecy, *Any more*
    than a handful and a guy's just being greedy. Not enough,
they whispered in corners, the word *whore* flitting

against orange lockers. Today, her father squeezes the last
    of the suds from the ends of her hair. Her eyes are closed,
so she does not see the bubbles spill into the basin,

desist, how her father's hands contract and expand
    in the water. Small bowls reposition. He is giving her
the slosh and turn, ripple of the pool that washed her. She hears it,

even under the lamella of stillness. She will forgive him bodies,
    this girl dozing, her blood slipping down. She'll think
of his hands in her hair a year later when he is gone

from them. When he bundles up the pregnant woman,
    headed for Des Moines.

sneaking up on a wildness

There it is, third suggestion from the top, *Sexual*
intercourse releases endorphins proven to alleviate
headaches. And since some people are kinder than others,
my husband decides for my sake to give it a shot.

I have quit red meat, yogurts, feverish reading, dark chocolate,
plus any kind of rock and roll and my tolerance for new
remedies is low, save the vapors of an extravagantly hot bath
and enough organic greens to start sprouting myself,

though those were suggestions one and two,
neither of which have stopped the elephant from
sucking on my eyes, one at a time, his tire-sized
feet cinching my head like a June gourd.

So we go at it when the skies change,
ivory clouds of pressure moving up and down
my spine—chased away by fingers, urging each small
knob to perk and snap while we roll around the living room,

family photographs and an empty cup teetering
on the coffee table. I am willing the gristled stalks at the base
of my neck, the rigid bulb of my skull to snatch up hormones
whistling through my endocrine system, their tiny, fiery,

edges to snip the stitches of ache. I cheer my adrenal glands,
their black-red rippling, *Go on! Siphon every electric drop!*
And how about that, in each room my neural synapses,
their bright white lips, too, saying *Please, Yes, Pleeeease.*

But my elephant gets jealous: his huge ears flap over me like sheet metal
and when my husband comes home I am like to kill him, piquant and crazy
with pain, pulling off his pants and my tongue across his throat and just yesterday
he said, *Baby,* he said, rubbing my hands rubbing him, *maybe we should get you*

to a doctor. This hurt my feelings, after all our hard work. I thought
for a few minutes, this man stroking the bell of my hips. *One more
week,* I bargained. And since some people are kinder than others,
he kissed my mouth a month-long kiss. *One more week.*

Tonight, his breathing soft blue and steady, I reach
from behind, palming the web of his sternum, his ribs,
down, down. Across the city, under an ash tree, my monster
also sleeps. In my bed I feel smart, strong and lean, godly.

I am sneaking up on a wildness. It is good to feel this way, the weight
of love sprung deep in my chest, spreading headward. It could be enough.
Only—I can't help it, I can't help it, I begin to chew gently
the flesh of my husband's ear. *Maybe,* I whisper, *you are a doctor.*

MY HUSBAND GIVING ME
A BATH

I remember doing this for fun—you'd lead me
to the tub with candles and foam, undress me, and always

the water would surprise me, as if I'd expected something else
to fill the tunnels of my ears, my hair mermaiding until

you'd tug me up, begin with crevices of propriety, soap
your way down. I'd like to think you still enjoy it, dimming

the room, and, really, if the light wasn't so, I wouldn't see
the steam rising from my knees and this breast I keep

a careful eye on. I haven't told you: this
is the only place my body feels right anymore,

the inside of an egg being kept warm by something
that wants it to live. Yesterday, I worked so hard to get my shirt on,

only I was too tired to pull my arm through when I realized
it was backwards, and when you found me sleeping

with my stupid elbow strapped to my ear, it made you laugh,
I'm glad it did, but it scared you, I could tell.

I could tell anyone who's wondering: it's *a bust*
to maneuver that single boob like an old glory, silly

when the rest of me is lumping up under this and that organ
for you to bend and kiss the one nipple still intact. Bless her:

the last thing intact around here—the boys might as well be home
for holidays, their playful wreckage covering the place. Today

I spilled capsules, teabags, pictures from the album, stationery
and that lamp I tried to reach but threw a book at instead. Oh,

those boys were such dirty things, I loved it, I'd use a handful of shampoo
between the two, scrub them good, squealing and squirting each other like
    dolphins.

Speaking of mothers, it's still a miracle yours stayed the week,
though she almost went home after somebody's Kleenex sifted through

an entire load of laundry like a burst of fusty petals. Her hands
work differently than yours, but when she rinsed my hair it felt like you,

balancing my head in the crook of the elbow, my hair so thin
she had nothing to squeeze water from when she was done. You know

I've never seen her like that, tender in her efficiency. I didn't tell you
this either: she insisted on shaving my armpits, though I

never bother with what's there, and it tickled me so, we both
got to laughing, like drunks, we laughed so hard. I thought you

might walk in and see us like that, her head in my armpit. I wanted you
to see it, I wanted it to be something you remember,

the way the body, even undone, offers itself to joy.

on Learning the percentage of non-professional head and neck massages which do not lead to sexual intercourse

Today I learned the word "uxorious," which means
  you love me to absurdity, but having your scalp rubbed I'm not
surprised. I mean it's about as sexy as mixing pancake batter,

Then I stopped talking because I noticed a growl
  coming from you, full-of-beans, and fingers scuttling up
the base of my neck, my hair pulled through your knuckles.

But wait, I said, *this bird's on a wire.* And you know what you said,
  or rather you sung, *Back home again in Indiana with my freckle-faced*
sweetheart eating salamanders on the banks of the river

where once in a while we'd neck. No, I'm mixing it up: that was
  my father last summer when he told me over the hospital
phone's crackly line of the tobacco leaves turning high yellow

and how dead-quiet it could get at night, all but the monitors
  which kept a rhythm to the songs he made up for Mom. What I
remember next is a buss on the mandible, the hush your mouth

sent out, the column of my neck humming like a grove of locust.
  You pressed your thumb behind my ear so close to the brain
I swear I felt it in my thigh. I decided or tried to decide, *This is*

ridiculous, the moon of my head in your hands. Then,
  as happens with those you have not been able to hold onto, something
else came to mind my father used to say: *Takk for alt,* with his chin

in certain rhapsody, like when he caught the biggest
  brown trout you've ever seen and let it go, this absolute
briefcase of a fish slapping from my father's hands into the water,

Takk for alt, he said, his smattering of Norwegian like lumps
   in a sac of lung: *Thanks for everything.* This is what I said to you,
do you remember? Then, our bodies proceeded, yours and mine,

sure as the deer from the thicket reaching the road to lick at salt.

santo domingo full of song

Here your language is worth nothing. Your tongue follows you
hesitantly, six steps behind, *conchos* honking, boys on mopeds
careening back and forth from the plaza. You should, you know,
billow out, out to all the sights, spread a pink fan from Santiago.

You will eat mandarin oranges and fried yucca for lunch.
You will touch the bright purple flowers in the tree.
You will hold your skirt at Boca de Diablo, its terrible
wind rushing out of rock, waves.

Still you will be a blank woman, unsure as
your fingers counting out the soft, threaded pesos.
When the roosters start, calling to each other across
the city, you open your body and fill it with their sound.

Another hour and you will hear the swung iron gates,
car alarms, flurries of birds, a frenzied dog, the proprietor's
merengue, the woman who shouts from the alley,
her enunciation slapping like a perch in your hand.

What will matter is the tough sun, your pineapple juice,
the balcony window, barred. What will be forgotten is just
beneath you, your hands limp on the sill, a sudden love
for people you do not know, cannot, will never know.

Even now, memory is a broken puppet with its strings across your lap.
Wait long enough, though, and the mountains come to you.
You find their green particular, held apart from the land
like a mouth holds its socket of speech, its beak-full of song.

FIrST CHILD, In THE WomB

We brought him from our skins, wet and black
    as a spoonful of oyster, his tips of fingers, his knees,
tiny round buttocks, grainy on the monitor:
    smaller than small, perfect as beads of wax,

every syrupy portion a gift of our equinox:
    your white thread of joy, my dim, open palm.
I am thinking now, after the doctors
    have told us the child will not live, no amniotic fluid

in his purple pocket of nutrients, no kidneys,
    that we should not listen to their sad, stern voices
telling us to terminate. We can hope
    he knows us, feels us holding onto our skins again

in gallant necessity, the coda of parenthood
    whispering like lips against a dark circle of blood.
Our own four kidneys, strong faces of water
    and electrolytes, push at the window of blue-black night,

waiting this miracle, the kinetic art
    of prayer falling carefully from our mouths,
my five months of belly convex
    as a warm egg under your hands.

Only the sweet birch is honest with us, its leaves
    brushing the glass near our bed, its branches are rhumb lines
pointing heavenward. You kneel against me
    in our desperate posture and fill the soft tunnel of my body.

Every Dance with Caroline

You don't think of it until this brown head disappears over the fence
you are running beside. You hear him say, *Sounds like you want some*

of me!—and then a hard laugh, the kind your uncle
gave last Thanksgiving about your acne, said he was only

kidding, the kind you feel behind your breasts, near
to the ribs, the small capsules of shock that, for a second,

make it hard to breathe. You keep running, veering away
from the tall fence, the sound, now, of a buzz saw. You

are twenty-plus blocks from your house, somewhere
between Cullen and Piedmont, far enough into

your third mile to feel the asthma speak her language of panic,
the air going in as gasps, coming out hums and moans.

You've not thought how it must sound to others, how unfamiliar,
how acute, to the mother with a baby pouch hooked over her shoulders,

only the tiny white arm of her child flopping gently
from under a checkered blanket, their black dog panting

two sidewalk squares ahead. Or to the older man, a fishing
hat, a clear plastic umbrella hooked on his pants, whistling

something Ella Fitzgerald with his chin to the sky. And there,
you feel an anger trotting beside you, near the clouds

of your mouth, the thick body asthma shakes against your face.
You understand vaguely it is not anger at the boy who said

this thing to you while cutting his dad's dogwood branches,
it's just this: *everything is about sex?*

But then, even that: the word *about* is not enough. Perhaps it's not sex
everything is *about,* but the white magic of anonymity, the power to throw sex

on someone as she passes by a loosely planked wall, never
looking in her eyes, not like the men in the truck who full-neck turned

to watch you cross Justin and Arroyo Seco, when you saw the calm
eye-whites of the man behind the steering wheel. He didn't smile.

Grass grows in the cracks of the sidewalk, crooked, insistent, and you
    understand
you are not angry. You are so close to home now anyway, you called it

the *homestretch,* back in high school when the coach, his mouth a pink
pocket, shouted from near the finish line, *Kick it in Kick it in Kick*

it in! No, you suppose everything is not about sex. Instead, the woman
stopping in the park, sitting on a bench washed in sunshine, unpouching her

baby, letting its small lips peddle against her breast, the old man walking
slowly, remembering every dance he had with Caroline, how malleable

she made him feel in those polished shoes—it's everything wanting
to be alive, wanting to be awakened, wanting to know it is part

of the day—even if that part is to watch a girl run, watch her
go, hear her pull in troubled air, the same air that easily swabs your own

mouth. You look at the sidewalk, following it, pushing
your skin forward. The green handwriting says, *Go. Go.*

GOD IS THE Dream

I. YOUR LOAF OF BREAD

Just for practice, let things rot. Leave
the bananas on the counter. Stay
the gerber daisies with mold
in their dark sockets, the baby
roses damp with age. Let it
push out from all our peels.
On your loaf of bread, green-black dust
like a breath of coal. On an orange, spores,
spilt like tiny white thoughts
from the tough, wrinkled head.

Can't you feel it, this possibility of life
springing helpless and bold across our kitchen,
writing its language on the husks and skins,
which are also the inside of my mouth,
taut and cool, waiting, which is also
the palm of your hand.

Hold to the marble top, love,
let the subtle bruises of our bodies
rise and brown, the spots of age
mistake themselves for joy. Just
for practice, stay with me, pushed
close to the bulbs of openness. If it
is enough, slowly softening, hour
by hour, day after day, remember
that we were children, we whispered
silver hairs into the air, held the block of cheese
to the light to see its fuzzy cover.

II. BOWLS OF MY BODY

We could stand
and flip pancakes over the griddle
all night, speculate the robins,
the albino squirrel, their precarious
caches. We could watch the line
of shadow sift up on the wall
of the barn, like a gray lake rising,
the eye closing, a slow lever
ticking shades of yellow up, up.

Instead I will go to the porch, let you
finish the plates of batter. On this side
of the house God sits with me,
swinging like we care, working
the nausea of the day down to my feet.

The bricks are speckled, the black
spider unhurried, the sun to the tips
of the trees now.

How is it all our dry moments
come together like a field,
spread before us heathered and barleyed,
aching for the mind to run through it,
aching for anything to set us to tears.

Love could be made to steam,
could be made to turn
and brown. Only, the sun has set and here
I am, my shoulders mottled with knots,
willing the bowls of my body to fill.

III. HOLY

It is September and the earth is waiting
for us to find her, all the corners of longing
chamfered, all the leaves
in silent, excellent suspense.
These years together are a fruit,
and our children hang from the branches
in my belly. Our years
together will fall from the tree.

Tonight, I pray us a long, long lovemaking.
At the end of the black sky,
I wait for you in our bed. Here is how:
you will turn off the light. Nothing
will be said, except you will know
how strong my heart is working in here,
and you will not fall asleep.

What can we touch?
It is tremulous here, in our
orchard air, you finishing your book,
me, marauding the spirit of Midas:
I turn you to gold. Only it is not
gold, it is warm like flesh and together
we hang, suspended against the other, we hang
and brown, our bodies awry with love.

God is touching us, the pillows,
the purple-black frame of night,
the pungency above the grape arbor, God is
the dream charging from your body into mine,
God is my hollow bowl holding your gold.

We can touch anything now. And nothing.

Your hair hanging down, your mouth a stunning insect
spread across your face, opening its dark wings,
it is only you who can speak.

IV. THE FEAST OF US

Even the short, deadened nights
are a beautiful bird to me.
You, here. Me, here.

I think of the rounds of air, circling
our home, the backyard furniture,
the clothesline I've never used, all the cedar
trees voicing complaint in the wind, the coyotes
answering with the moon.

Tomorrow I will go in again,
they will slide the microscopic camera
into my navel, seek and eradicate
those dark places of tissue piled up
against the organs. I am not rotting,
the brown spots inside my body,
I am not rotting: it is only fingertips
of a joke, those chronic cells *de trop*.

I tell you it is the kitchen of the body,
apricots, pears, plums in her baskets,
a cup of salts in her cupboard,
she meets you with a vase
of New England Bluets on her shining,
moist countertops. Nothing has been
thrown out, only sheltered variously.
Nothing has changed but the stripes
of grime on the linoleum, wiped clean.

Somewhere we are laughing at this,
somewhere we are trying again
the wide rim of the future, the sure,
candle-bright spoon lifting
into the feast of us.

IV

HOUSE OF BREAD

TO Prayer

I.

Your hands are quick and free, one day crossing the harp
and one day the loom, neither of which you heed enough. Your hands
swim the long bowl of some shore in America, which itself
is a kind of shore, spooled by a dark set of longings. You

are almost rotten through with a love you cannot name. Somewhere,
someone thinks about crying, someone fashions a sloppy basket,
someone enjoys an afternoon thick with wine and slabs of rye.
You hear these things: guitars, crickets, coughing, half of August

in a day. Hands cannot hold these things as surely
as ears, and blood does not belong in either
but in the lissome cup of the body, its hollows, its handles.

II.

Today you press them together for anyone who loved Jayjay Escolar. The men
who killed her had hands like yours, they gripped her shirt and bowed
her neck, opened her legs, cracked her jaw. Hands will take an eight-year-old
on a shortcut home from school. If the ribbon of splendor unfurls

in exact amounts, you hold the sounds of *rhododendron*
among your teeth and brush your wrists over campanulate flowers,
all the showy clusters her mother mentioned, all the leathery
leaves. Your fingers are steeple-stiff, your palms fleshy

as a California peach. Your mouth pleads the small bird
back to God, your tongue a rapid wing. This is the quarter moon
you never saw, the brush soaking in thinner. This is the body
that breaks, and today it was a Filipino girl you did not know.

III.

Were you with her? mapping a new way home from school,
maybe humming something you thought she knew, unclipping her hair
as she turned another corner of Baguio City. No, you were not
there. You're still in the chapel, opened or opening. These

are seeds on your face, and you know you have done
your work. Your hands are bones, rivers, conundrum: the patter
of knuckles on the pew. Jay-jay-Jay-jay. The old sun sliding down
your chest, the old sky, fingerprints on a pane you cannot touch.

ACROSS THE WORLD A MAN IS LIFTING HIS GUN

Across the world, a man is lifting his gun,
and there is nothing I can do but sit,

here, the grass limbed with shadows from the trees,

the sounds of birds overlapping
the sounds of other birds—bleat, chirr,

trill, caw. Thin-legged and slight-breasted,
hope is one of these, chimerical,

set all morning the voice to swinging out, swinging out,
since only the silence is a chaos, laced from the sun.

I hear, across the world, who
is alone: *alone* is a gun pointing

in his hands. What would tell his fingers *No?*

Surely—this, the salted glen of notes
risen from throats smaller than

a thumb. It's become important:

their noises, their calls gently orbiting each other,
revealing their spaces in the sky: *We are here*

with you. Redbird, grackle, chickadee, bobwhite,
finch. Together say *Existence.* It trips finite

from our openings, and O—how the calm

seems stuck here, tall stems musky dry, crepe myrtle
blooming fuchsia and the chimes of someone's heart

so loudly means, indeed, *indeed.*

MUCHAS GRACIAS, MY LOVE

I.

In Houston, awaiting your flight—you have been days
in transit—you try to wash your hair in the bathroom sink,
you are bent over. The slight strain of water stops and starts.
It is an automatic faucet, quick-spouting, parsimonious,

its red eye does not acknowledge your head. Your hands shake,
frustration seeping through your grip of the trivial. The earth has become larger
for you and still there is the trouble of water—the planet has run a shining
across your body, and of all things: a faucet and water.

II.

In Nepal a woman closes the eyes of her son. It will be
days before her fingers lose the feel of his lashes, prickled as the tip
of wheat, whispered shut. In Seoul, a man must decide who he loves,
that simple, horrific selection. Guatemala, and a peddler of bracelets takes

your quetzal, slowly, turning over strands of color in her lap so
that you, too, might be beautiful in the fading light of Lago de Atitlan.

III.

It's true: countries outsplay their four to six sentences from the guide;
countries mark themselves by the puckers of their currency, the customs agent
who examined your pairs of underwear, one by one. The toothless man
singing, his sitar hemorrhaging in the stale air of the ports. You

have never been more sure of stillness than in flight over Thailand,
each hour a child in your lap, slack, sleeping. In your dream, the silent
dance, the bamboo aftershave you bought for your brother,
the people of each place more real than your own hand, pressed
to the scalp. As you wake, bamboo sprouts in your soup.

IV.

A woman who cleans the bathrooms brings a cup. She has come
out of nowhere, speaks no English. You are grateful, *Gracias*
sits easily on your tongue, *Muchas gracias,* the cup in her hand,
your head again in the sink. And as the water streaks over your neck

you feel the woman's fingers, working the shampoo into its tepid foam.
There, your face in the white bowl, her hands in your hair, you
are saying *Thank you Thank you,* you cannot stop or switch to Spanish,
and now she is saying it also, *Thank you Thank you Thank you.*

BOCA CHICA, PLAYA DE REPUBLICA DOMINICANA

AFTER PSALM 93:3

It is here you know how innocuous your Indiana heart,
chamber of leaves, hickory shells, old, wet newspaper. Here
you find the tell-tale fins of *los tiburónes* thrilling
out in the blue plashes. No one screams.

One thrill is like another, you'd guess, as fragile as sugar packets
between your fingers, twisted empty, each forgotten with the ticks
of your wrist, the tongue's pleasant swipe. You might be allowed
your imbecility against the noises of Boca Chica, her hospitable

hush,   hush,   hush.   But you didn't come to be comforted.
Let's say you have left someone. Or someone has left you. The white
battering sun teases this out in waves. *The seas have lifted up, O Lord—*
Let's say it was never about someone. Was it? Yes. Was it? No.

In the raw squint of day you won't lie: you want comforted, you always
have. God's fingers are in the water, *The seas have lifted up their voice—*
tickling the hard gray bellies of sharks. For a moment you miss
the exquisite quirk of a word like shark in Spanish: it will translate to *fish*

and *swindler* and *expert.* For a moment all you can think is your stupid
wet feet, sucked into dark sand, your toes burrowing beside sand dollars
in their muck-homes, your body falling slowly from your mind, a dark
and muck of its own. *The seas have lifted up their pounding waves—*

Let's say who you are is situated enough. Choose which cloud
to follow and your neck will turn of its own accord. Choose *tiburón*
or *estafador* or *perito* and there in the slow-rising bubbles of your heart
you'll only have plunked in the ocean a toe, all flesh, uncanniness.

THIS IS JUST a SUGGESTION

Invite me to an apology, this soft thing: the accordion
    spread of a peeled tangerine, bright skin still under
my fingers, scent on my wrist. How about my

watch. I left all those stupid hours in your
    hands. You must know it feels superficial, asking
my watch back, uninvited. No, come to think of it,

I won't. You won't be there. Then the drive home,
    arranging pillows, picking at a verse, looking for the sliver
of stamps that always falls in the crack of the desk.

You want me to say it? I'll say it: It's been bad.
    I'm a bluegrass ballad, crying splendid and a minute
too long. But, you know, *enjoy* the sorrow. Admit

there's this limp, patchy pleasure. There is. We could
    laugh, begin with something easy. Here's easy:
say who it is when you call, your mouth with its

oblique consonants, a coconut hoary in my hand.
    Is it enough to say *I once chased across the sky,*
I once was a particular bird, impenetrable? Look

at all these wings, and only one
pecked-clean cloud. Just look, would you.

unearthing

I.

The wide-faced man in the coffeehouse, late into the night
with his cigarette and double-shot whatever, cornered
her against her notebook: *Talk about a good writer, now Henry
Miller is the shit,* he says. *He's a loser, man. Writes such beautiful
stuff.* He starts in: *Wanna know how I got successful*

with women? Later she tells Miguel of the man, she works
across his back and laughs insipidly, *He was reading* Casanova.
Miguel holds to her calves, smiles with his tongue behind his teeth.
And when she dreams, finally, against the small, raspy breaths next
to her, the man's face appears, eyes too far apart and lips a shade

nearing eggplant, again he speaks to her: *So your
man, he likes smart women?* His cigarette burns
slowly toward his hand. Next morning the slatted sun
reminds her of her father's recording studio at the back
of the house. Towers of compact discs, the spooled cords,

delicate metal of jacks, the clicks and silences, her
father's voice low and opulent across the insulated walls,
citing St. John of the Cross and John Donne. He
administered spankings there, in the studio, the sound
of flat slaps fell on the floor like a linen slipped

off the table. Always the dilatory lecture. Her standing
with hands behind her, palming the stove-hot buttocks, hiccups
deep in the folds of her throat. She first heard Bach and DeBussy
in that place, the efficient trills of Noel Paul Stookey,
Joan Baez, Van Morrison. *We believe all in one God.*

II.

Isn't it Someday yet, Someday with all those old
words she told herself, consoled herself with, the swell
of them marveling up in a cloud over her head. *Distract me,*
is what she's really saying to Miguel, *let me love you to distraction.*
She could swear it isn't insipience keeps them together,

the twain (ah ha!) *shall meet,* the concurrent intelligence
she is almost willing to forget (*How brilliant would our
children be?*). It's not dimensions of the body that distract,
but the *way,* isn't the sequence of parts, but the faction.
The tongue against the teeth, how he says, *My people,*

and Peru is less a place and more a door, hot oranges and pinks
of his knit hats lining the shelf, a cluster of fingers against her
breast, Andean lutes from the speakers and forgotten potatoes
on the plate that never were, *silly Irish,* from Ireland. Every russet
inch rests, patinaed, in his and her lovely (what some would call)

bipartition. It isn't Someday, but it's perfect, the darkness.
How anyway she closes her eyes with talk of God. When
the home of his mouth slips open to her, ceilings rise with a company
of angels, anarchic. In light air and black air, the process of reverse
osmosis, carbon filtration, ozonation: we are purified water.

She realizes the voice saying *You like it?* and again,
You like it? is hers. They laugh at detumescence.
They debate if the plants have not grown or not grown.
Pebbles in the bamboo's jar lay against each other, each ring
of the young bamboo growing carefully out in S-curves.

III.

At the Madison Library, she reads Yeats: *When you
are old and gray and full of sleep,* and a pigeon accompanies
Liszt in "Sospiro," moaning unreservedly outside the window.
Its groan filters delicate and grave into her headphones
and it could not matter at all the orange-rimmed eyes,

oil-blue body. *Murmur, a little sadly how love
fled.* From the 4.100 aisle a man approaches slowly,
says, *Have you been told you have the most amazing
blue eyes.* He holds folders and a book, she thinks most likely
he is selling something. *No thank you,* she says. He nods

toward her hands. *Poetry. You know, I love Jack Kerouac.*
Before he walks away, tall man in semi-pressed clothes, he
drops his number on the table. She will demarcate the use
of *shadows* in this poem, absentia and mythos, before
she stands to stretch, crumple the man's offering into the trash.

She does not mind. It is something in the rows of books,
the long dusty lives of paper in this place, she is sure, the same
synergy as his fingers scraping at her jeans before dinner,
the light falling sideways out of reverence for words, every
movement of Rachmaninoff, Ennio Morricone. Of course

a man is overwhelmed. She is only basket-full of the essentials, here,
in a chamber of minds. *And what happens to truly beautiful women?*
She thinks each man will catch his own symbiosis, she thinks each new
day, received as it is, is underrated. She thinks spines should not be allowed
to disintegrate. She thinks the word *demarcate* is probably overdoing it.

IV.

Every time she hears Van Morrison, she is in love.
It has to do with the numinous held in his mouth, it has to do
with reaching the country of her father by boat, skiff, canoe.
Tonight, after reading a chapter from *Eat Right For Your Type,*
she feels especially fond of *Best of Van Morrison, Vol. II.*

Every man must own this CD, every man must read with his knuckles
on his cheek, every man must hold still when the firefly lands
on his forearm, allowing the woman with him to cup the place
and watch the yellow-green pulse on their skins. Every man must
spill a little chocolate ice cream on a woman's leg, right above her

knee, use his tongue to wipe it clean. Every man must let a woman
quiver against him when news of tumors in her father comes over
the phone. Every man must talk with her the stars, the supergiant
only visible in September, the three months when Jupiter appears
before Venus, the constellation of misunderstandings left behind in love.

Tonight, yes, alone for an hour, she resists lighting a candle.
Instead, she takes off her clothes and reads the snatch of a psalm
her mother printed on a postcard: *O give us help against the adversary,*
For deliverance by man is in vain. Through God we shall do valiantly,
And it is God who will tread down our adversaries. In the sonorous noises

of middle evening, she knows she has, by default, orchestrated years
of longing a misnomer, the daughter of a woman who loved her man too much,
the woman who cried before and after her first orgasm, she thought the cock
worked against the man's mind and the woman's body. She lifts his name
from tongue to God. Last night, again, she laughed with Miguel inside her.

V.

When she hopes he is indelibly hers, it is only by means
of this word hopes. When she was seven, her father was spraying
for termites and the cask of poison exploded on the left side
of his body. For as long as she can remember, he has not complained
of the blood clots, unexplained fatty tissues, arthritis, cardialgia.

For as long as she can remember, she has wanted to marry a man
like her mother. Sans compliance. Sturdy patience. The clean
frustration, all those soft skins of the palm. So she wears the cuirass
of loving quick and loving hard, and never knowing anything about love.
The wide-faced man said, *I started getting women by pretending I was dumb.*

Only once did she take a stranger up on his haphazard offer: *Tomorrow?*
We'll go for a walk. She'd borrowed his dictionary, this man with a tall
cup of tea, Beckett in his hands, questions in his mouth of faith and luck.
Days later, she'd memorized the small mole equidistant from his chin
and bottom lip, ellipses of muscle rounding his brown shoulders.

He would not take the sex she offered in soiled, rich handfuls. *You wanted
to be married, remember?* She felt him hard, felt him reposition carefully
away from her. His valediction meant, *I'm thinking of you, you know.*
The slatted sun in the morning reminds her of her father's recording
studio at the back of the house, sets of heavy earphones, a wire

hanger squared and covered in her mother's hose in front of each
microphone, the switches sliding under her father's fingers. He showed
her his Bible in this room, margins in Proverbs, Isaiah, Ephesians where
he'd written her name. The Bible's cover was collapsing, the spine a soft
memory. Mary Chapin Carpenter sang through the end of the world.

VI.

Miguel refused to take a camera to Machu Picchu, knowing the tip
was his mind's, set against the sky, the colors of *his people* sold in fragile
booths along the way, his mother clucking discoveries, kneading ancestry
into peripatetic moments with his sister, winding trails up and back
from the fingernails of God. *It was discovered in 1913,* he told her, *back*

when people still discovered things. Deep in the morning,
when all the water of earth is fallen, falling, even though she hears
the voice spread across the room of their bed like a thin canopy,
Cover me, love, I'm cold, she does not know it. Or, at once,
she knows it so completely she does not know it at all.

FOR THE MAN FROM PERU

If this were another time, I would greet you
with a small bowl of limes, quartered, stark

as the face you wear to kiss my fingers. If this
were another time, I would rustle the shirt

from your body, note the black drop of mole
on your shoulder, your skin smooth as a spoon,

lean, worked over and over on the fields, from me to Arequipa
to Colca Canyon and back to me again, your eyes roaming

the side of the roads for a branch of wild kumquat
to bring through the door. If I could hold you

and say, *This is mine, mostly,* and keep the guerrillas
in your country distant as the taste of white wine,

Hugo Avallaneda Valdez at-large, who, save the papers,
is to say the quarries will not open again?

On the day you squeeze dry a lime into your mouth
no one will speak *El Niño* or *Asian financial crisis.*

You will shake your head and grimace, the glands
at the back of your mouth tight with joy,

what even I and the coca leaf could not give.

TO JILL BEHRMAN, NOVEMBER 2000

*"The search continues for Jill Behrman, a 19-year-old IUB sophomore,
disappeared May 31 while riding her bicycle. . . . On June 2 her undamaged bike
was recovered 10 miles away from her route."* —Indiana Daily

Last weekend my husband and I tucked flashlights
    in our heavy jackets and called for you at Salimony Resevoir,
where once a snake crossed in front of me and I screamed. This time
    my voice was steady, braying in a pattern against the snow. Still,
it was panic pushing out the sound, a solitary vision of you,

though we have never met. My aunt says you showed
    Lop-Eared Rabbits in 4-H, worked at McDonald's, rode your bike
each morning. She said they found your helmet by the road
    in front of their peacock pen, your 12-speed a hundred or so yards
from the east gate. Though we are three hours,

exactly, from Bloomington, we had to look in the places
    you might be. The whole town and now the whole state wants you
back: divers and driver checkpoints, off-road crews and dogs are on
    your trail. I hate to say it, but mostly we are scared for ourselves.
Women carry pepper spray and mothers hold their children

pinchingly tight. Today, I saw you on the billboard, six months
    after you were plucked from your bike, and I thought you
should know: from Madison to Mishawaka, we are searching the thickets
    and ditches. Last night I asked after you in my sleep,
Have you seen Jill Behrman? You might have been there. Sometimes

though, and I'm sorry for this, I forget to pray, and most often
    I cry for myself, which is to say, I will go back to Salimony
and if I think of it I'll shout, *This is Indiana!* our borders
    the heartland, yes, here Jill, a certain hub, working hard,
as we have learned to, land and wind clotting

each season, the blocked sun all those winter months, Jill,
    we know what loss is, and so we look for you, even if
the billboards peel. Somewhere inside us the shock
    does not wear down, not like the nub of hope: they have found
the house where your blood whipped in small spots on the wall.

It is hard to know which questions to ask, since I grew up
    like you, feeding rabbits, lobbing acorns at the barn. This must be
what terrifies us, how near you are, how near you have to be, a state
    you can drive top to bottom in five hours, four across. But perhaps,
too, it is how near we are to them, one way

or another, those who have taken you. When I pray,
    this is how: they leave you clothed, they treat you better
than I did my favorite corn-shuck doll, tossed across the room,
    mashed into corners, left on the floor for the more boring days.

TO JILL BEHRMAN, MARCH 2003

"Hunters in a remote area of Morgan County, near Paragon, stumbled on human remains, which have been positively identified as Jill Behrman's."
—Indianapolis Star

You need the field to let you go, you need your bones back,
the bending marrow of recollection, like my friends, who say
    I remember you talking about this, and *Didn't you go looking
for this girl?* In Texas, where I have lived for two years,
        where bones all the time are blowing with the dust back to the sun,
Scott phones, then Gia, to tell me what they have heard on the news,

    that their boots tripped over you, *near Paragon,* the filthy irony
in a name, in the acid that rose from their stomachs and swabbed
        the backs of their tongues when they understood they would not
be hunting any more that day. Surely they wore orange vests,
    Carhartt hats, had pocket warmers for their hands, and here is the part
that matters, standing over the mound, were they holding shotgun or bow?

    Think of it this way: trees, too, make us stumble, their roots
jarring up from the earth, as does a single-brick headstone laid out
        for the soldier who died on Indiana ground, knolls of clawed-up soil
where moles and crawdads also fought for territory, the stumps
        of old clothesline poles and the last block of a leveled silo, these and even
a bramble of Johnson grass, the reconnoitering that snags our feet,

    unwitting, like the remains of a girl who went for a bike ride three years ago.
It isn't true I left and never looked back, though I almost forgot that rise
        of horror like a grackle's bark and the long months of its echo.
I have always had those dreams, long vans lurking, someone's sock
        in my mouth and hands achieving an Indian burn on my ankles
or the tops of my knees, bodies that smell like blacktop and skunk.

And if this were about me, I could shudder and somehow fall asleep,
the laudanum of finality like acres of winter wheat at the farmhouse
    where they ran to phone the authorities. But this is about the field, the last place
your body knew. This is about the frosted bones, the land that cried *beauty*.
    You need our small faith upturned, you need the decomposition of queries
launched skyward, falling back to faces that waited, ready ourselves

to shout *This is Indiana*, since only your body was honest with us.

we take the sky

We take the sky, as if red is something we could own,
something we might find in the stillest moments,
as if the earth is humane and wouldn't break
our bones. (None of His were broken. Not one, allegedly.)

Red is in the land too, is in the way we look at each other, the hardness
of our sleep, the need to fall down, to tell of the pox that swept Aunt Jess,
the drink that ushers Father, the path that never leads to wealth or rest
or health—but the one we always take. *Shalom,* we say. *Buena suerte.*

We always take the sky, fold it over ourselves,
the soil, run it across our skin and cling to it,
savoring the tart of a lemon, palming a bar of soap
even when our hands are clean, naming the insects

that fly across the white bulb of moon late at night,
rakishly loving the one who knows our smell,
saying (as if they are not questions), *Isn't this how
we stay alive* and *Why shouldn't I burrow here.*

This is how we drum on, cold and ungrowing—
what more to be than alive? It all hums: so we die in small bits,
so the egg-shaped hollow that sits behind our stomachs,
so He died and rose again on the third day, so (what).

We take the sky, we scatter on the land. We fall down,
grab the everythings, the tiniest cures, fall down again,
wash ourselves in red and know, unwittingly, it is not enough.
More certain than anything: it will never be,

and then here, in the stillest moments, the story rushes again
(veil splitting, stone rolling, Mary, Peter, John, running,
linen and spices like a limp cocoon, the blur of angels, the one red
splash of a second—like a rose breaking open—when we know),

and somewhere inside us a small green seed pricks the dirt,
coiling for air. He soothes and stirs, fingertip-sized holes in His
hands, roaming the soil and the sky for our broken bones.
And the shaking on earth is our brand new lives:

Alleluia, we say, feeling even the empty oval of our stomachs rise.

AFTER *The Virgin of Vladimir,* 12TH C., ANON.

I. DESMOND LEARNING TO READ

Together is the hardest word in the world
his finger   slowly rubbing across the letters

He sounds out *to get her*   and I   with pencil darkening
the base of *t* and *h*   say Well   but   these two are together

the word turning in   on itself   and all I know
is to laugh   since I have given it   away

But   he ignores me   his finger
poised on the spot where letters become sound

It's a hard word   I say   he knows what *hard*   means
He's a whiz at   math   can tell you seven times

anything   but reading   He's been home schooled
the supervisor tells me   only his mother

nearly beat him   to death with a high heeled   shoe
and more than once duct taped a paperback book

in his mouth   Tonight we are reading
about Halloween   *Jake put his   costume   together*

Desmond tells me soberly   Trick or Treating is from the   Devil
and I wonder in his small body all he knows of   God   the Devil

Last week   we read *Hansel and Gretel*   horrid mother
leading her children deep into the woods   to die   and Hansel

ever-resourceful   white stones   crumbs
hovering over his sister   and still   the house of bread   the witch

I hated to read that fairytale with him   Gretel pushing
the old woman into   a stove but   as yet he can't lament

the swallowing of prayers   pages damp
with saliva   on his neck her fingerprints

the corners of his mouth   stretched like a buttonhole
and she   saying   That's   my good boy

II. OUR LADY OF TENDERNESS

Christ Child with your arms around your mother
what have you done for us

to take in our hands bona fide conception with flesh?
Saint Catherine of Siena said

You drew us out of your holy mind
like a flower

and she was illiterate most of her life, her prayers written down
for her, and it is in prayer we have

two hands up, like your mother's, every finger the final petal,
not touching you but meaning to touch,

either buttressing or balancing stacks of tokens, glasses dark with wine,
our limitations and that hot need

to love. Did you think I wouldn't see it is you holding her,
not her holding you? For

she has already the unfortunate that-which-is-to-come in her eyes,
drooped with sorrow, our careful human sap.

You, as though you will breathe into her—if only to adumbrate
a Russian artist's rendering of hope—

you, a child who couldn't have been *only* a child, your thick neck
twists to kiss her, and she looks

vigilantly at us. Ocher walls, chipped and ancient,
they are not your home. She knows

this, she tells me, obstinate as I am, slowly broken down
in the bones with a weight

known only by leaping belief, she asks with eyes like grapes
not *what has he done*

but *what hasn't he?* O Little Panacea, suffering up under
your mother's brow, keep your hand

cupped close, bless her name when years later the crowd
will beg for your breath, hallowed and terrible.

III. HOUSE OF BREAD

If one small body, arms with fingers and fingers
with dirty quarter-moon nails, legs with knees and knees
with scabs, chin that tries out the meaning of *lift*, the body

undetailed by age but with existing, holding up an ear
into which I read slowly, the head I will put my palms to
with pertinence, optimism—that silent meat of *O I pray*—

if this small body understands itself, the dark life
of subsequence and causality, careening and folding
and speeching and fighting, what should it ask? Our short

walk from hope to failure, the rope of knowledge
thrown as far as can be thrown, any kind of nothing
consumed with eagerness—the stark release of *O I pray*—

Somewhere tonight is the passing of sun to moon and moon
to earth, but I cannot find it. Instead, this Mary and Jesus,
carried from Constantinople to Kiev, Kiev to Vladimir, Vladimir

to Moscow, its centuries requiring restorations,
but somehow (according to scholars) the faces of mother
and child *still those of the original Byzantine masterpiece.*

Perhaps this is what happens, given our resourcefulness,
crumbs, stones, laid along the dust of a crazy returning,
given our *togethers,* mothers and sons, sons and Gods,

the shaky unshakables of blood and divinity, the hardest
fusions we will never quite make, having long ago given ourselves
to doubt, having known with certainty not even our faces

will remain. Perhaps this is what happens, and all the while someone
has been singing *Ave Maria* in an old city, *Ave Maria* and the chained
women on a Georgia Sea Island shouted *Jesus been down to the mire*

You must bow low to the mire Honor Jesus to the mire, so here we go,
Desmond, the Christ, mother and mothers of all, me—*O I pray*—
Jesus been down all the way to blessed Bethlehem, *bet lechem,* house of bread.

Bardo · Suzanne Paola
Donald Hall, Judge, 1998

A Field Guide to the Heavens · Frank X. Gaspar
Robert Bly, Judge, 1999

A Path Between Houses · Greg Rappleye
Alicia Ostriker, Judge, 2000

Horizon Note · Robin Behn
Mark Doty, Judge, 2001

Acts of Contortion: A Book of Poems · Anna George Meek
Edward Hirsch, Judge, 2002

The Room Where I Was Born · Brian Teare
Kelly Cherry, Judge, 2003

Sea of Faith · John Brehm
Carl Dennis, Judge, 2004

Jagged with Love · Susanna Childress
Billy Collins, Judge, 2005

CPSIA information can be obtained
at www.ICGtesting.com
Printed in the USA
FFHW02n1619190818
47880767-51565FF

9 780299 212643